I0485596

Vintage
NEW YORK
A Trip in Time to a
Forgotten City

ISBN-13: 978-1519236456

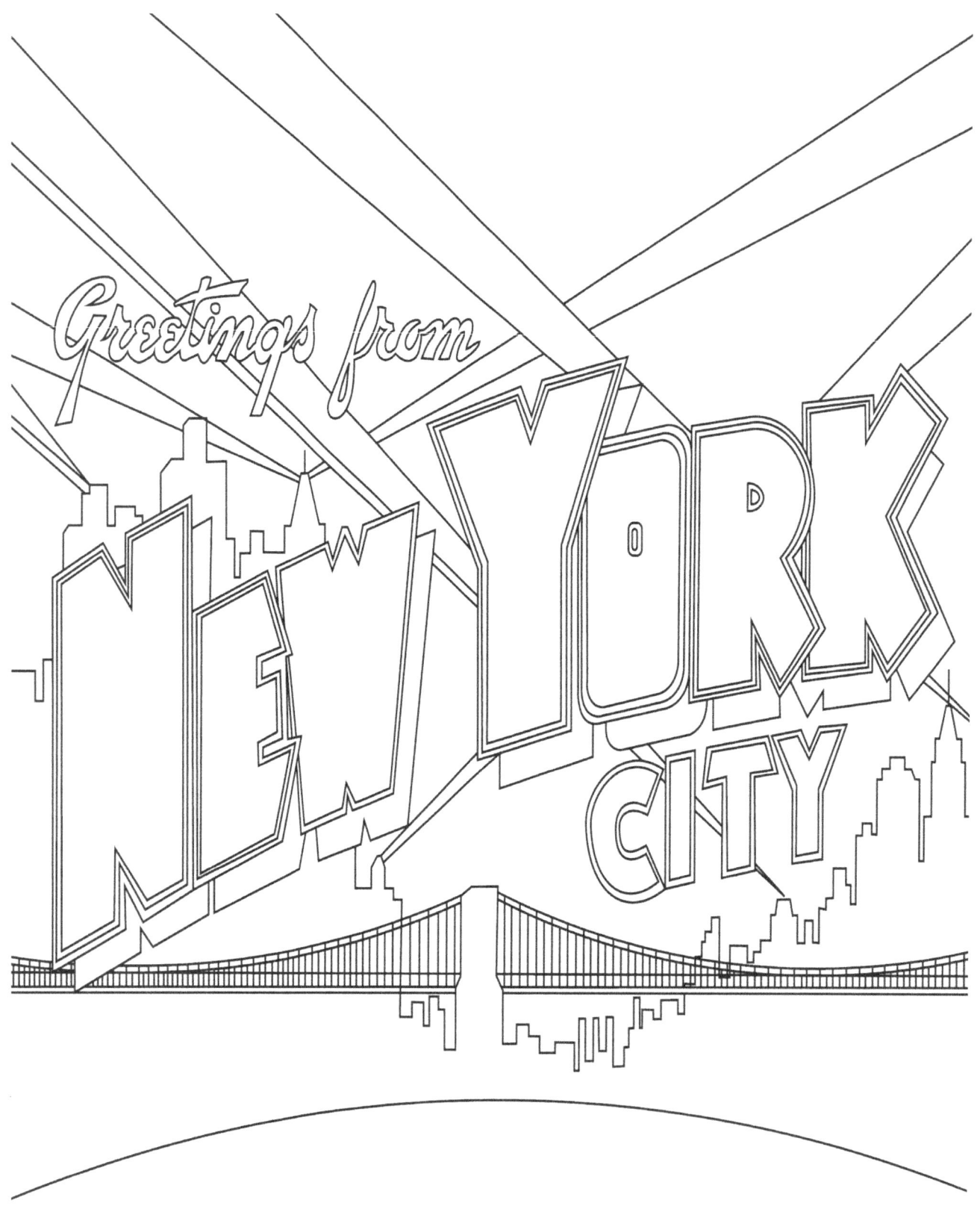

Greetings from New York City

New York City came to dominate American life when it began to consolidate from 1898 to 1945. This consolidation began with the formation of the five boroughs in which the total population was 3.4 million. In 1904 the New York City Subway and other transportation links opened and bound together the new Metropolis.

Catholic and Jewish workers increasingly emigrated from Southern and Eastern Europe. This expanded the labor force until the World War

The labor force increased and expanded from the many unskilled Catholic and Jewish workers immigrating from Southern and Eastern Europe until 1914 when World War ended the immigration. African Americans from the Southeast, as part of the Great Migration, began to head north because of the labor shortages due to the war.

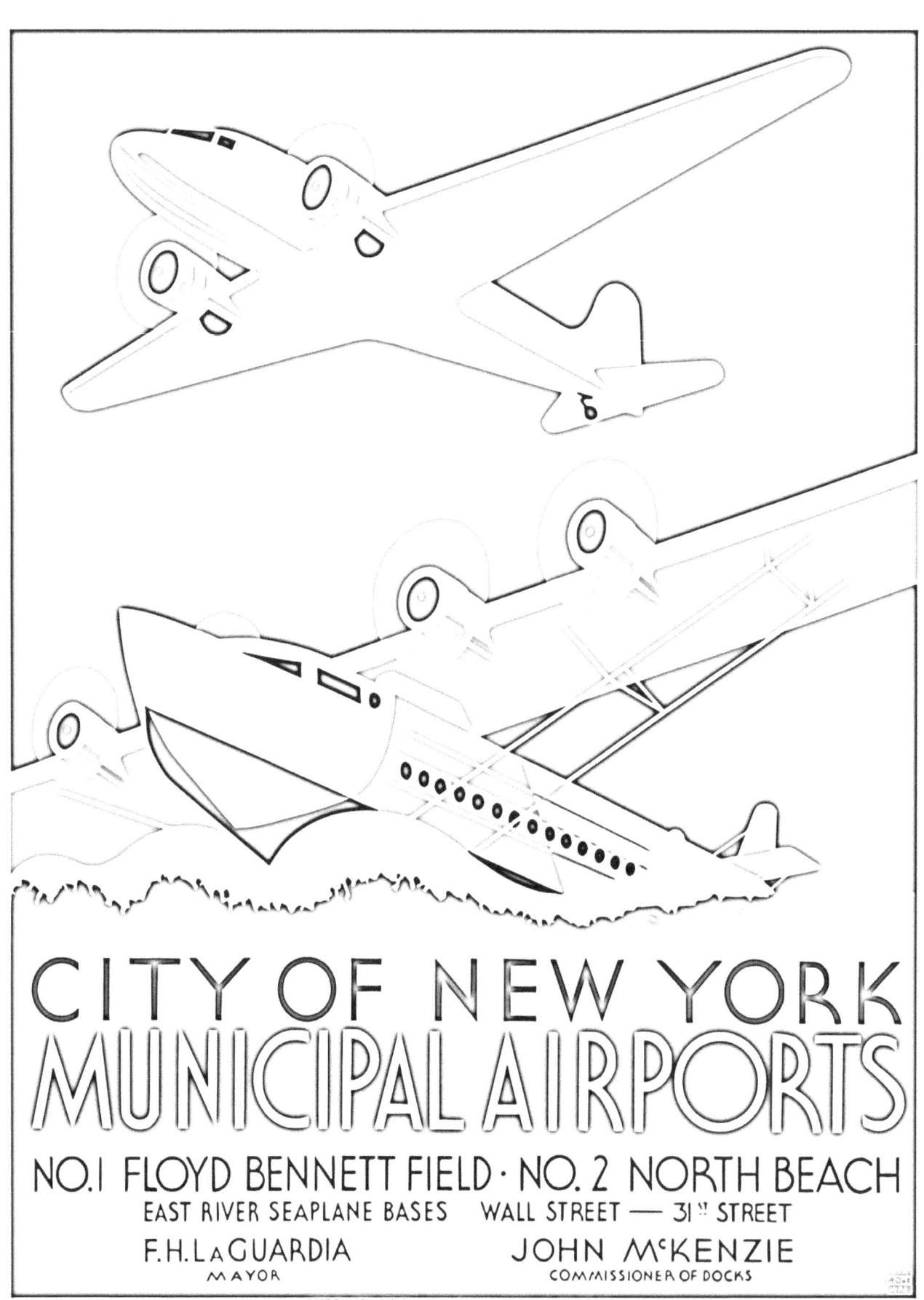

CITY OF NEW YORK
MUNICIPAL AIRPORTS
NO.1 FLOYD BENNETT FIELD · NO. 2 NORTH BEACH

EAST RIVER SEAPLANE BASES   WALL STREET — 31ˢᵗ STREET

F.H.LaGUARDIA
MAYOR

JOHN McKENZIE
COMMISSIONER OF DOCKS

MADE BY WORKS PROGRESS ADMINISTRATION · FEDERAL ART PROJECT NYC

City of New York Municipal Airports

The Floyd Bennet Field and North Beach are East River Seaplane bases on Wall Street and 31st Street, this poster shows and airplane and a seaplane. The WPA Federal Art Project in New York City created the poster to promote their municipal airports, circa 1937.

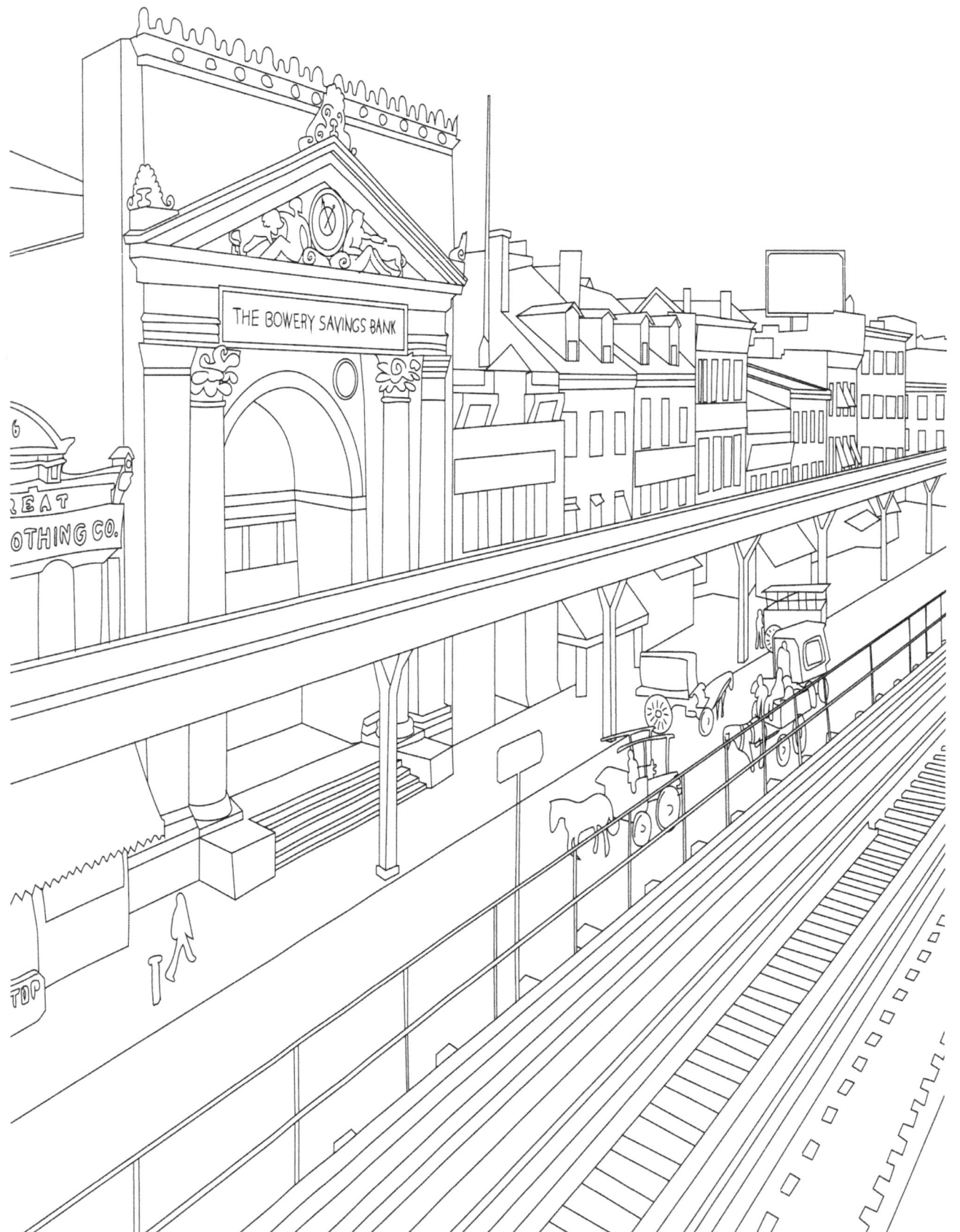

Bustling Bowery Street

The Bowery Saving Bank became the largest and most successful savings bank in the entire world, according the "1907 World Almanac & Book of Facts.

In 1982 the bank was sold to H. F. Ahmanson & Co., and was renamed as Home Savings of America. Later in 2002, the bank was no longer in service and instead opened as capital, where banquets and events were held.

In 1966 the Bowery Savings Bank was considered a landmark and in 1966 the beautiful interiors were landmarked.

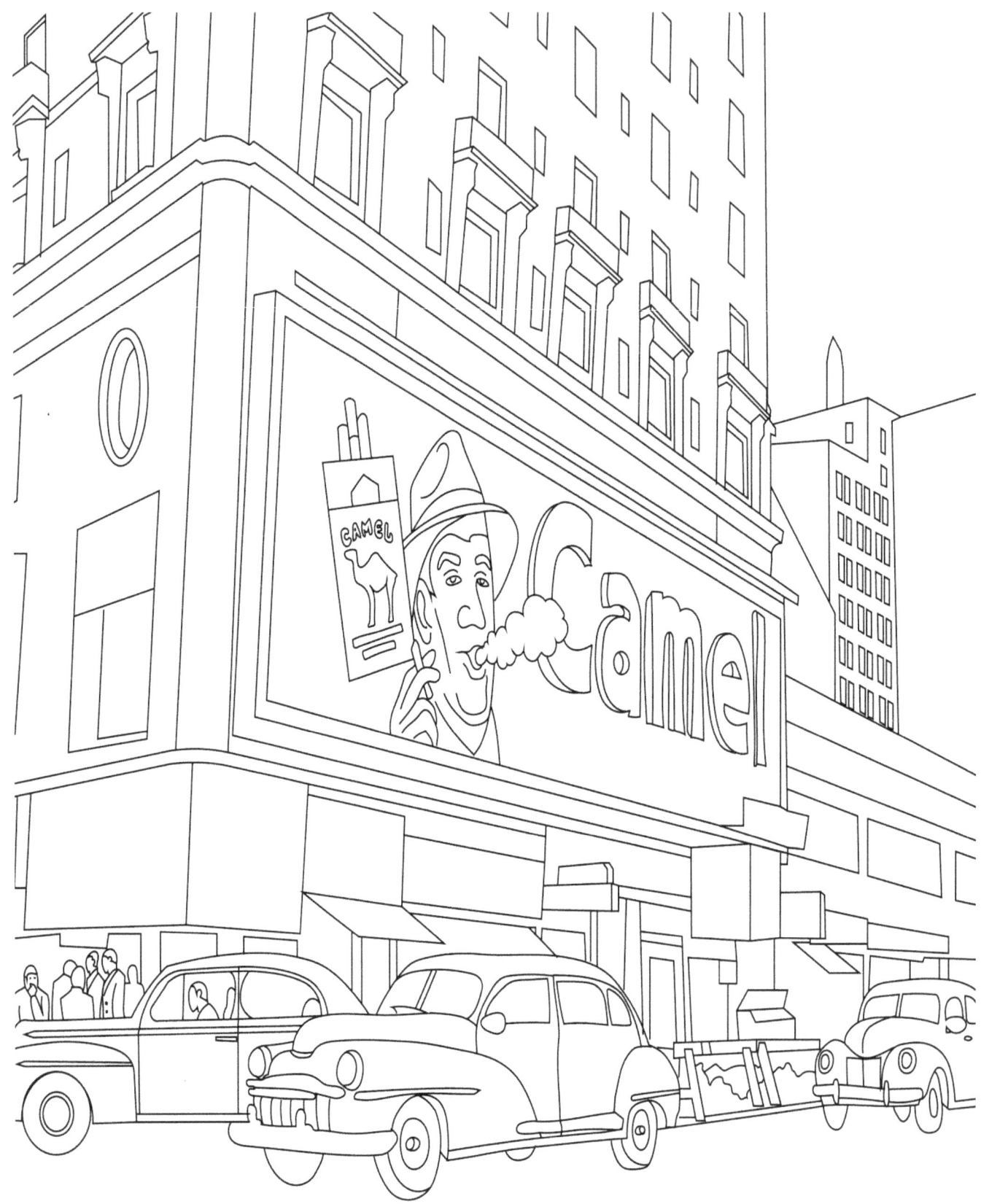

Billboard Advertising Camel Cigarettes

P. Lorillard and Company tobacco products were advertised in New York daily paper in 1789, and were the first known advertisement in the United States. At the time, the negative impact on health from using tobacco products was not known. Emerging in 1868 "Bull Durham" was a brand of tobacco known on a bigger scale in the USA, advertising how easy it was "to roll your own".

There were advertisements in full page, color magazine and newspaper in the decades leading up to the World War II. Slogans were created by companies and endorsed by famous men and women. Due to lack of information on health risks, the only opposition to smoking was from moral standards, which led to advertisements seeking to make smoking appear fashionable and modern to the public.

Many Tobacco companies sent free cigarettes to be included in the American soldier's C-rations during the World War II. The soldiers became addicted to the tobacco during the war and when they returned home they continued their use which led to cigarette sales reaching all-time high for the cigarette companies.

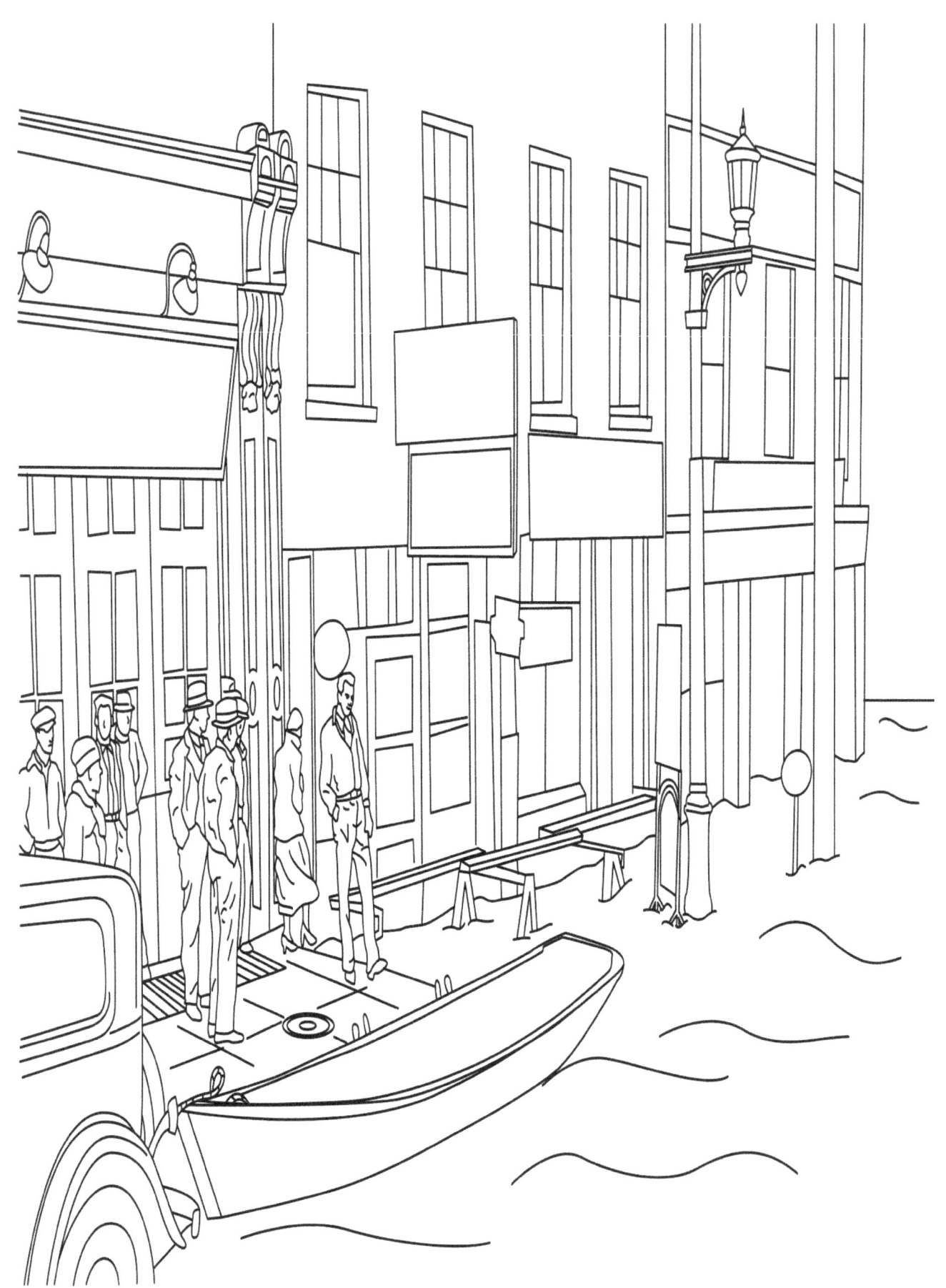

Flooded Street in New York

One of the strongest subtropical cyclones that hit Long Island, New York was the New England Hurricane in 1938. It was a Category 3 Hurricane on the Saffir-Simpson Hurricane Scale and killed more than 600 people. The remnants of tropical cyclones commonly produce heavy rainfall and flooding in New York.

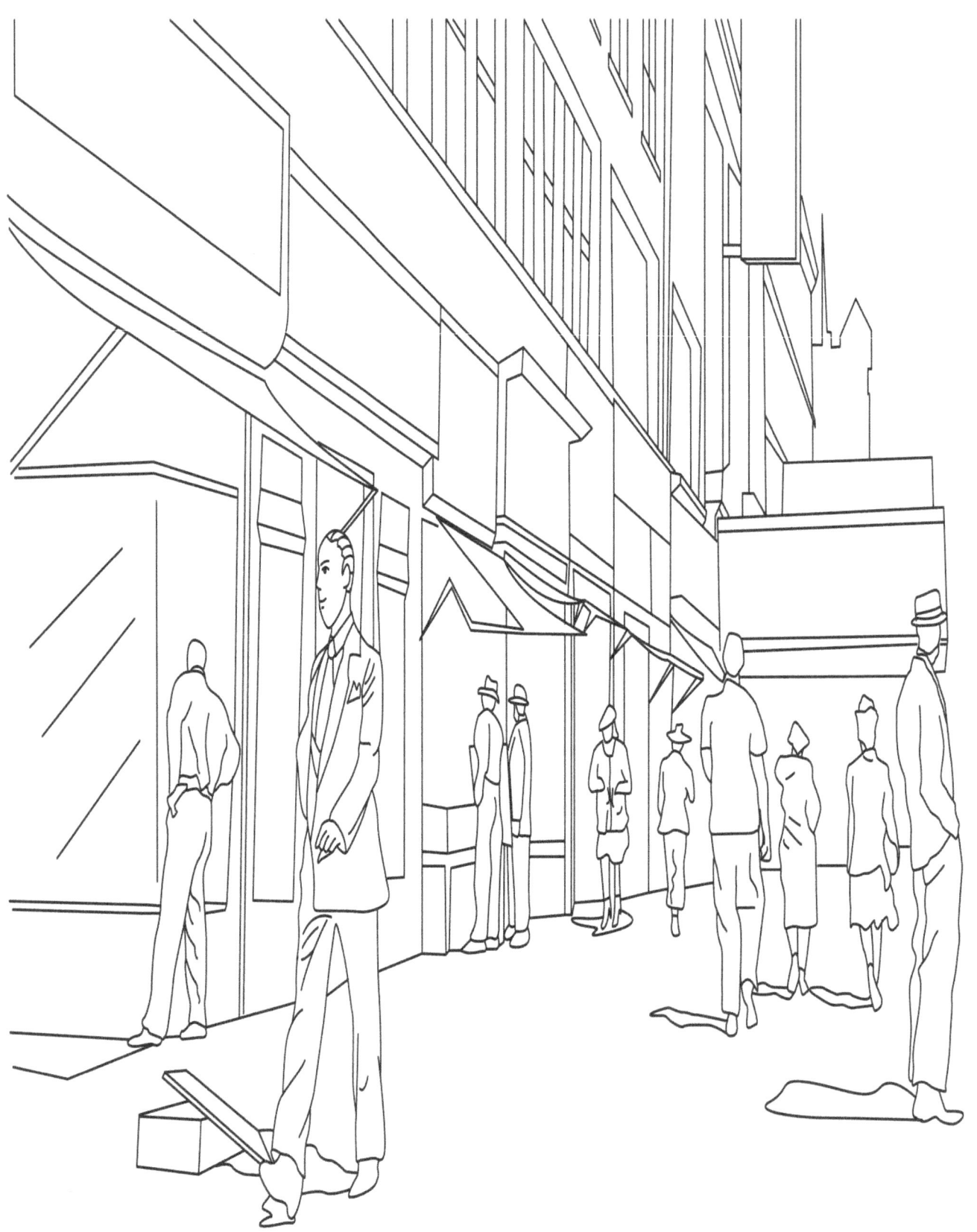

Streets of New York

The busy street corners of New York City have always been full of hidden treasures that would grace any home or wardrobe. Having museums and parks, sightseeing tours and concerts, film festivals, events and shopping, New York has been a place of interest.

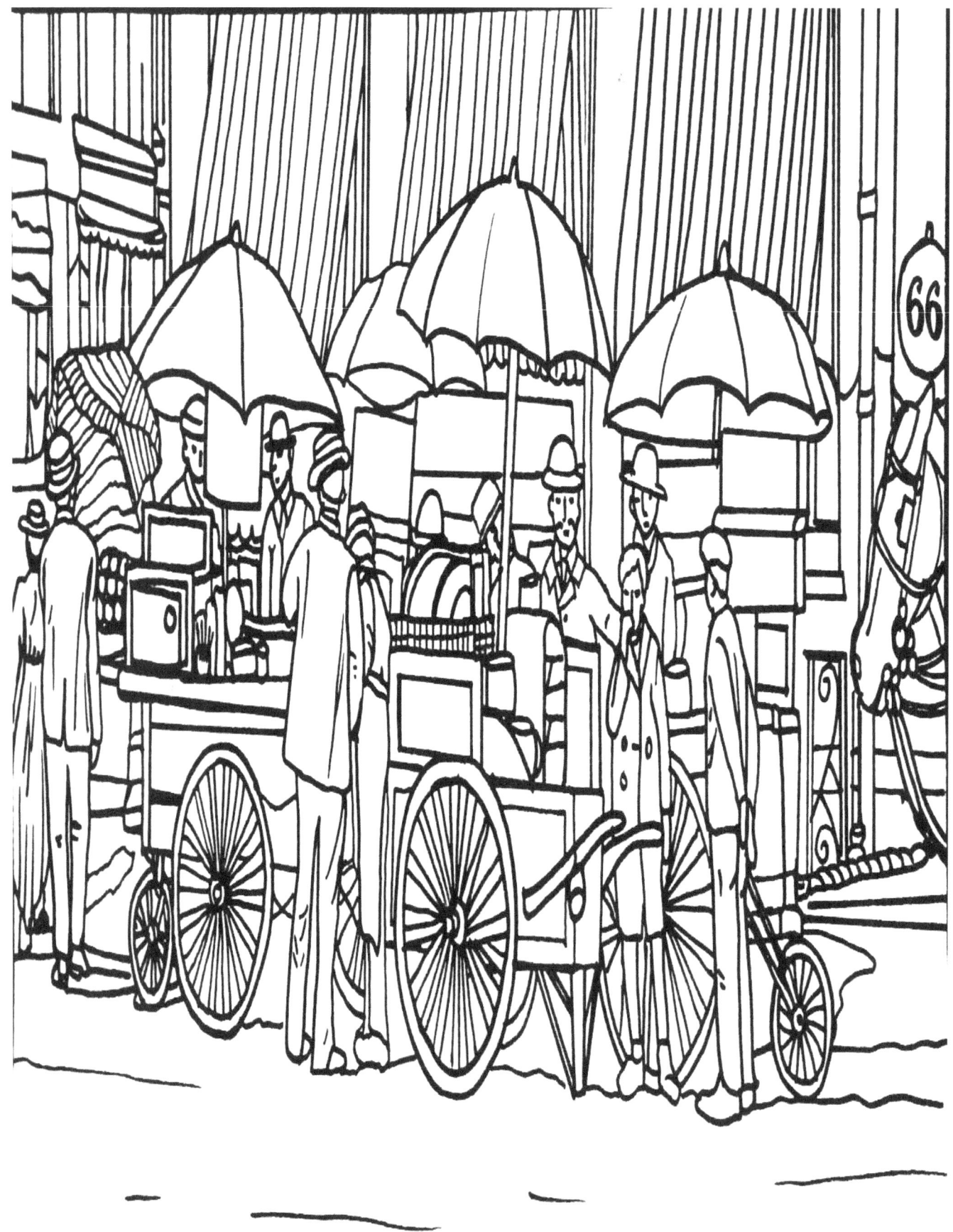

Lunch Carts on Broad Street, New York, NY.

Since vending from pushcarts has always been a great way for new immigrants to get a start in their new country, the food has changed with the wave of immigrant groups that have come through this city. The earliest street food was not hot dogs or pretzels, but in fact oysters and clams.

At one time, this was the food of the masses and even the poorest citizens ate oysters for dinner. As European immigrants continued to come to New York, the street food changed to hot corn, pickles, knishes, and sausages. In the 1970's and 80's, it was predominantly Greek souvlaki and kabobs being sold from carts. And then as the Muslim population increased, so did the halals carts which now make up most of our lunches here in Midtown.

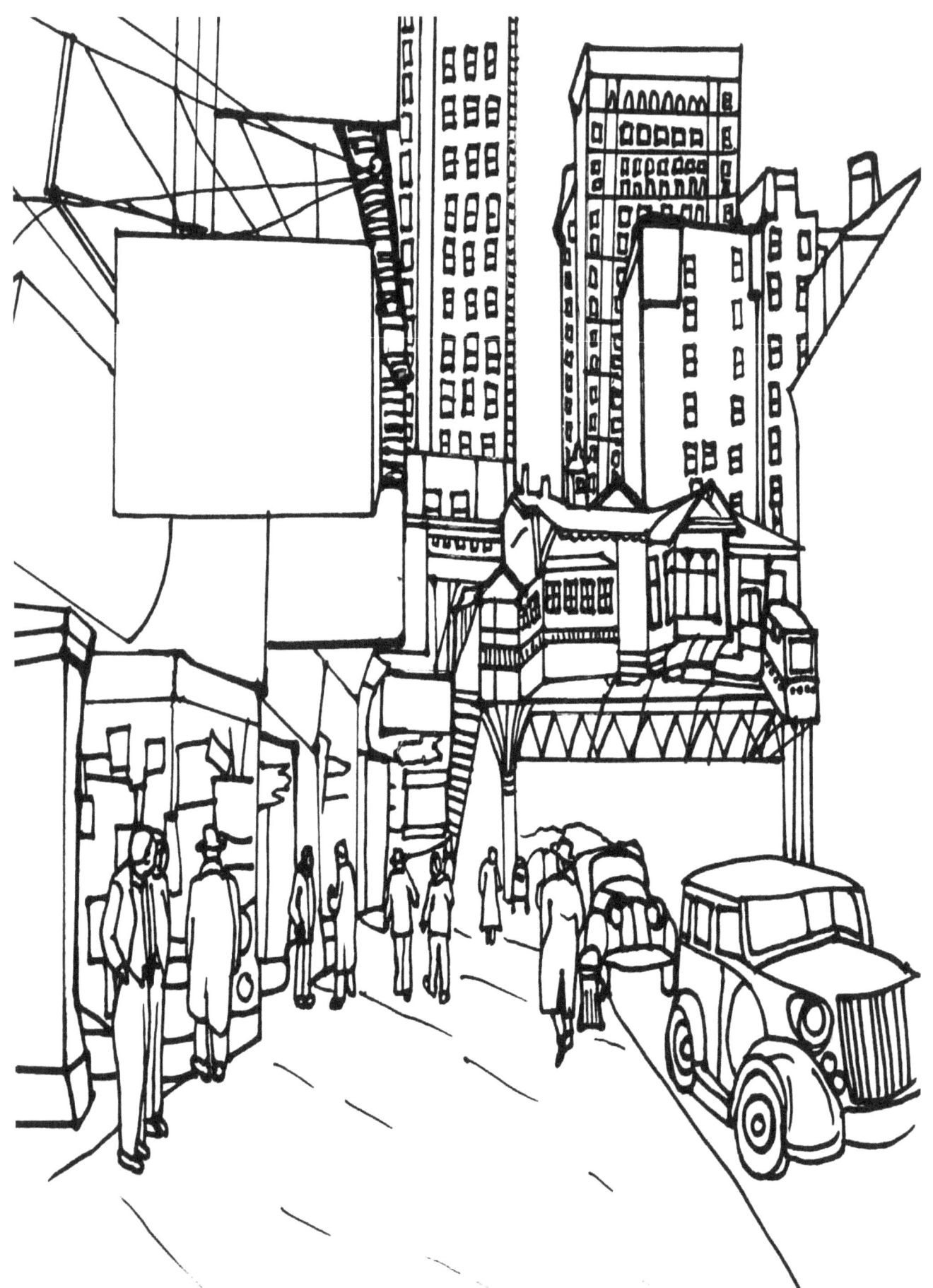

Radio Row

Harry Schneck started the Radio Row in 1921 by opening City Radio on Cortlandt Street. It was a warehouse district existing from 1921-1966 in Manhattan, New York City till it was torn down to be replaced by the World Trade Center.

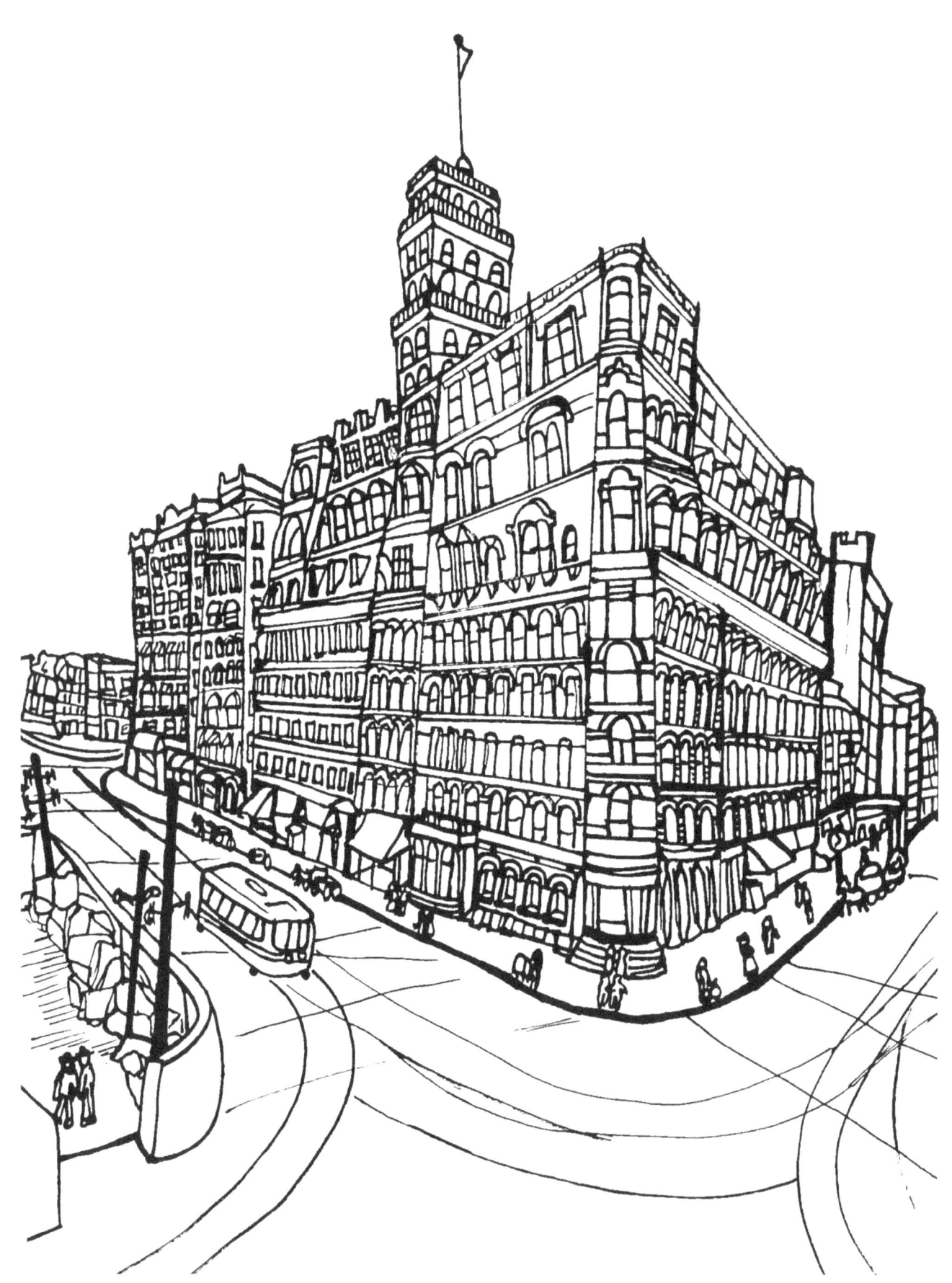

New York City's Grand Forgotten Hotels

Today, skyscrapers and office buildings stand where these beautiful hotels once were. In the mid-1900's most of these buildings were demolished.

The Astor Family's massive Waldorf-Astoria hotel had a successor "Hotel Astor" built in 1904 located on Broadway between 44th and 45th Streets. The Hotel Astor was luxuriously landscaped and elaborate rooms indoors. In 1950's William Zeckendorf owned the Astor, but went bankrupt in 1965 and in 1967 the hotel was demolished. The One Astor Plaza stands in its place today.

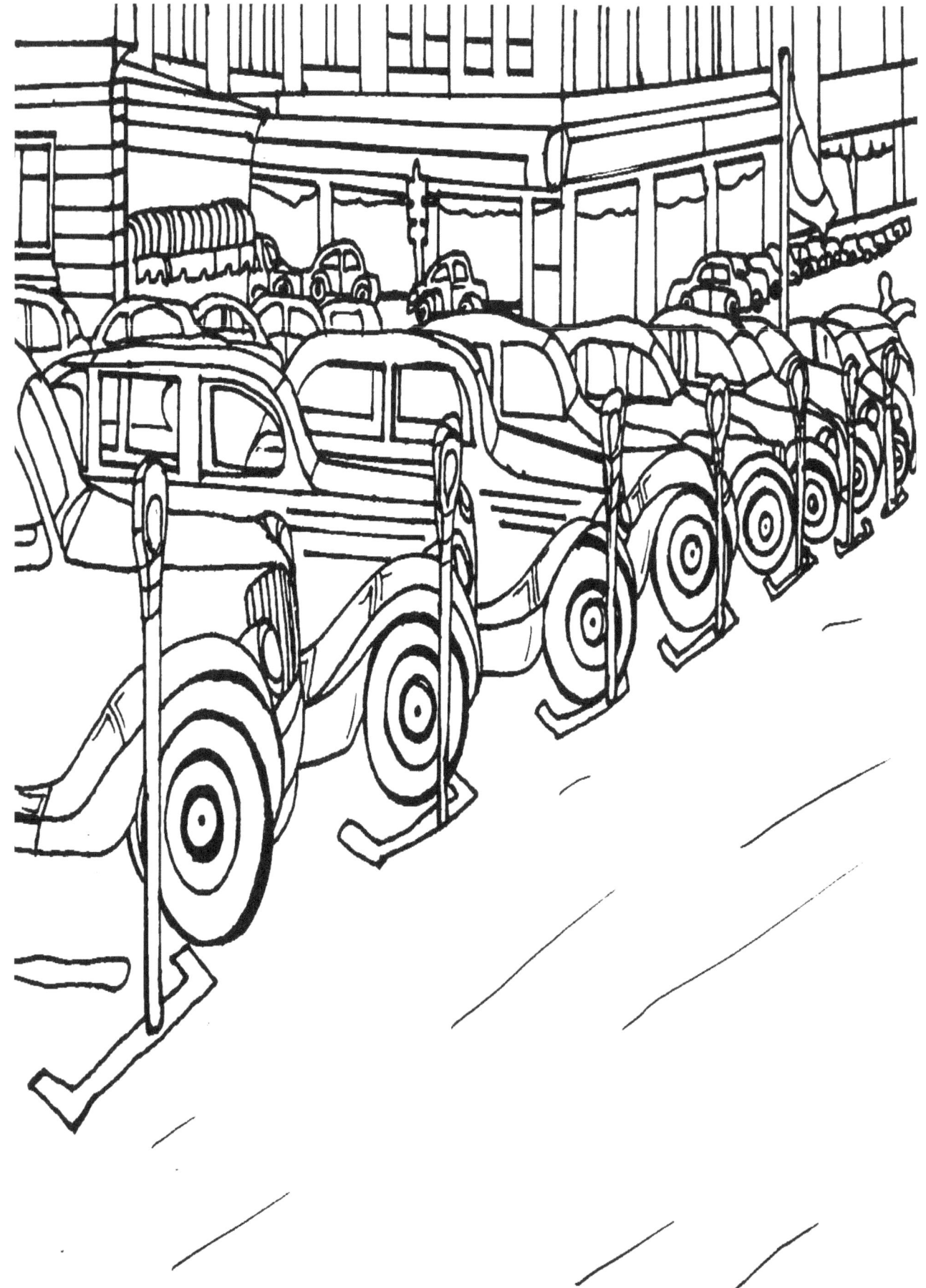

Cars and parking meters
1938

1940 brought in new styled vehicles including luxury automobiles; the Delahaye 135 convertible, Packard Clipper, Town & Country wagon, Chrysler Saratoga, Highlander, Plymouth, Dodge Luxury Liner Custom, Continental, V-8 deluxe, and the V8 Deluxe 4-Door Sedan rolled off of production lines.

These 1940 style vehicles had a lower, longer, broader and more massive look to them. During this time new vehicles went for about $800. On Average they got about 15-20 miles per gallon and you could buy a gallon of gas for $0.18.

In 1942, when World War II (WWII) was approaching, the production of automobiles for civilians came to a halt and resumed in 1946.

St. Louis, Missouri was the automobile capital before WWII but then later the new leader became Detroit, Michigan and remains so to the present time.

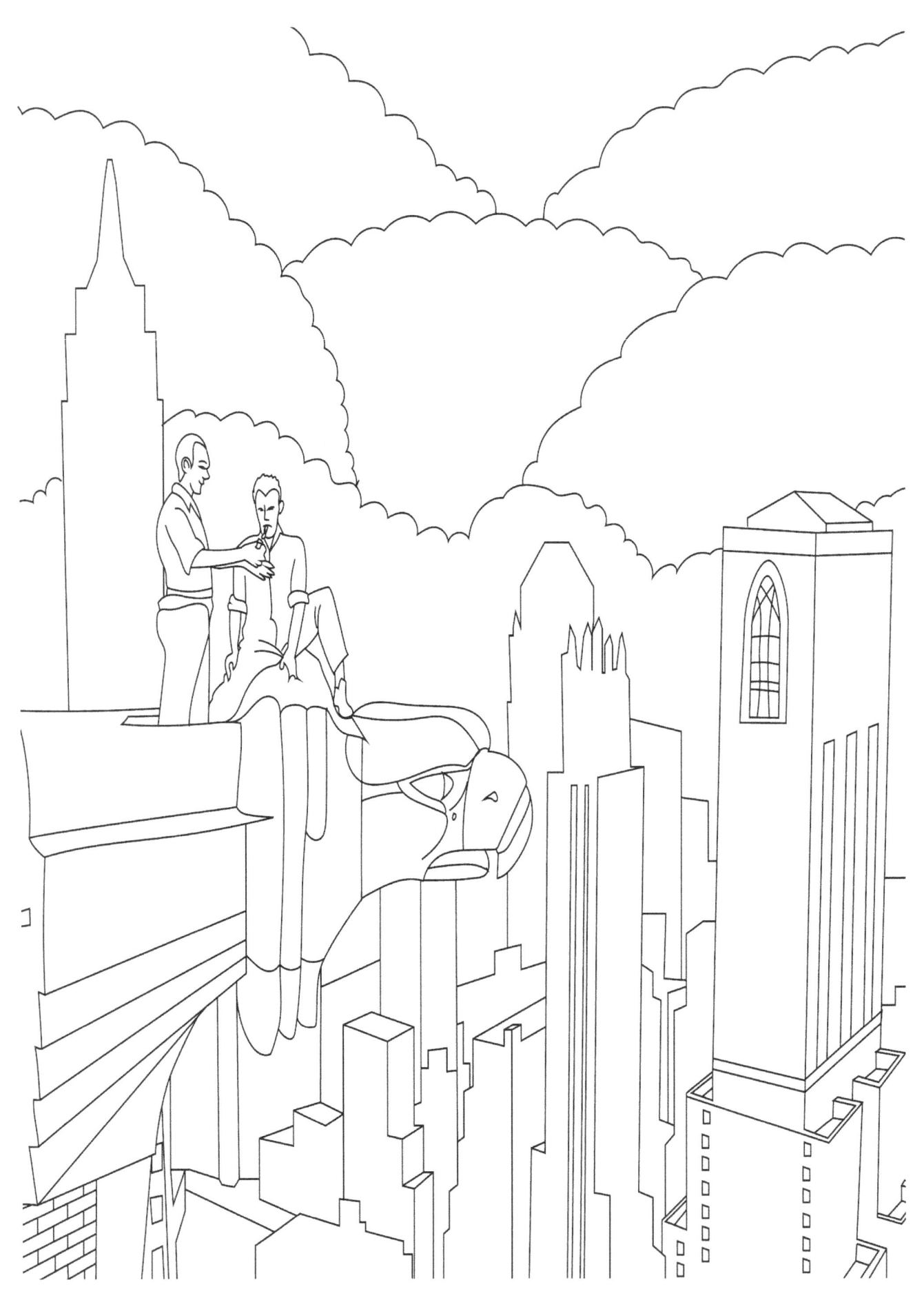

Chrysler Skyscraper

A competition began in New York to build the world's tallest skyscraper. The Chrysler Building was built at an average of four floors per week and it was designed by architect William Van Alen.

Van Alen originally planned a decorative jewel-like glass crown in this design. The base design was showroom windows tripled in height and, to create an impression that the tower appeared as if it was floating in air, topped by 12 stories with glass-wrapped corners. William H. Reynold disapproved of this original plan because it was too advanced and costly for him, so the design and lease were sold to Walter Chrysler.

Walter P. Chrysler worked with Van Alen redesigning the skyscraper adding 36 meters (118 ft) to the new plan. As chairman of the Chrysler Corporation, Walter planned to make this skyscraper their headquarters. The gargoyles and various other architectural details that were added later were modeled after the hood ornaments of the Chrysler automobiles.

Construction of the skyscraper began on September 19, 1928. To create the non-load bearing walls 391,881 rivets were used and 3,826,000 bricks lay manually. To coordinate all of this construction, contractors, builders and engineers and other building-services experts joined together for this massive project.

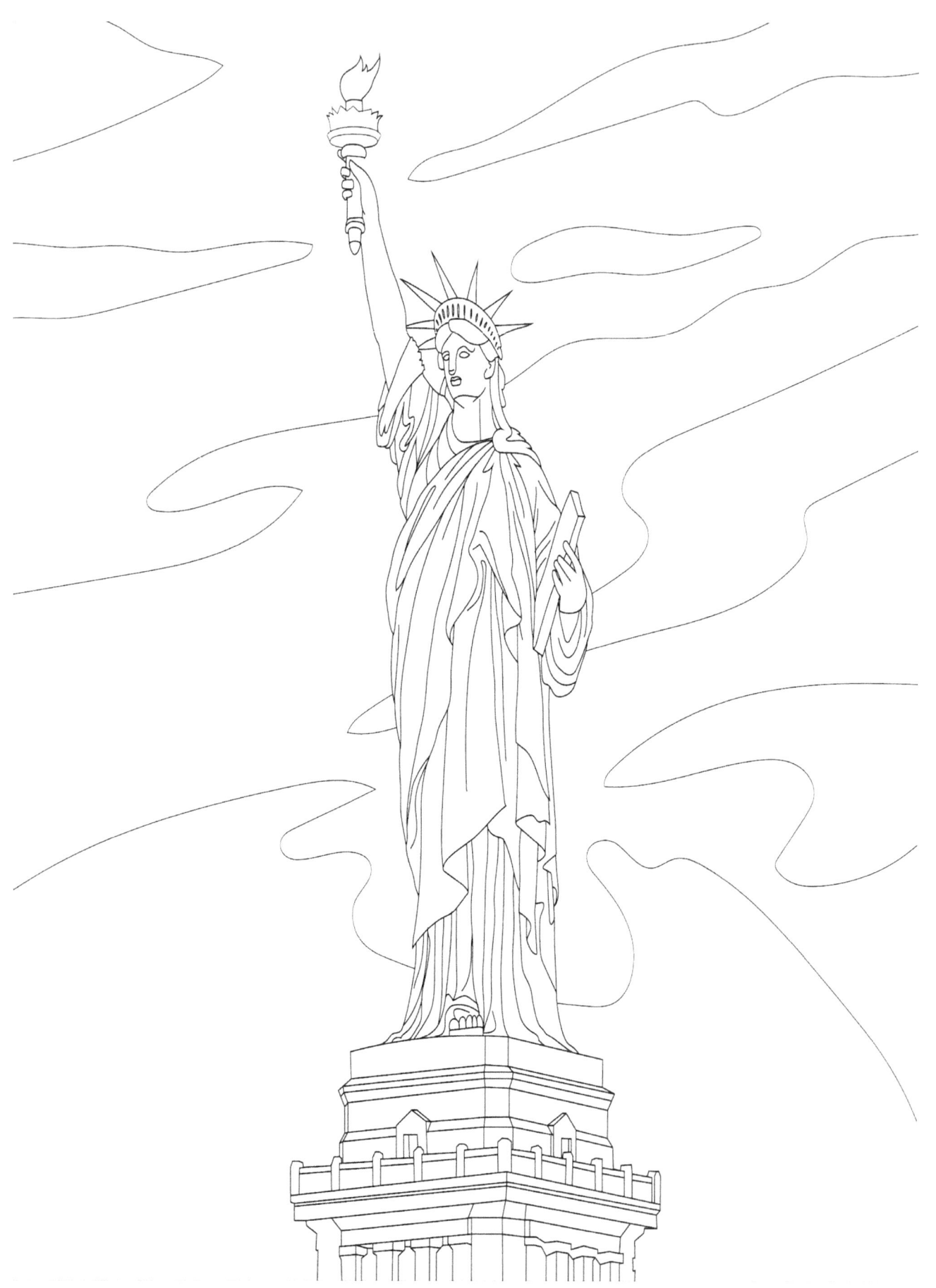

The Statue of Liberty

As immigrants arrived from abroad, the statue of liberty, an icon of freedom and of the United States, was a welcoming site to behold. A French sculptor Frederic Auguste Bartholdi designed the copper statue and it was built by Guistave Eiffel.

The French financed the Statue and the American provided the site and built the pedestal for the statue, as was proposed by Edouard Rene de Laboulaye in 1875. Before the designs were completed, Bartholdi built the head and the torch-bearing arm which were exhibited publicly at international expositions. In 1876the torch-bearing arm was displayed at the Centennial Exposition in Philadelphia, and from 1876-1882 it was displayed in Manhattan in the Madison Square Park.

The Americans were having difficulties raising funds to build the pedestal and by 1885 work on it was threatened. Thankfully more than 120,000 people, most of who gave less than a dollar, were attracted to contribute to the project being inspired by Joseph Pulitzer of the New York World.

Finally the Statue was finished, so France shipped it over in crates and assembled it on the pedestal on the Bedloe's Island (as it was previously called). President Grover Cleveland led the dedication ceremony dedicated on October 28, 1886. It was a gift to the United States from the people of France.

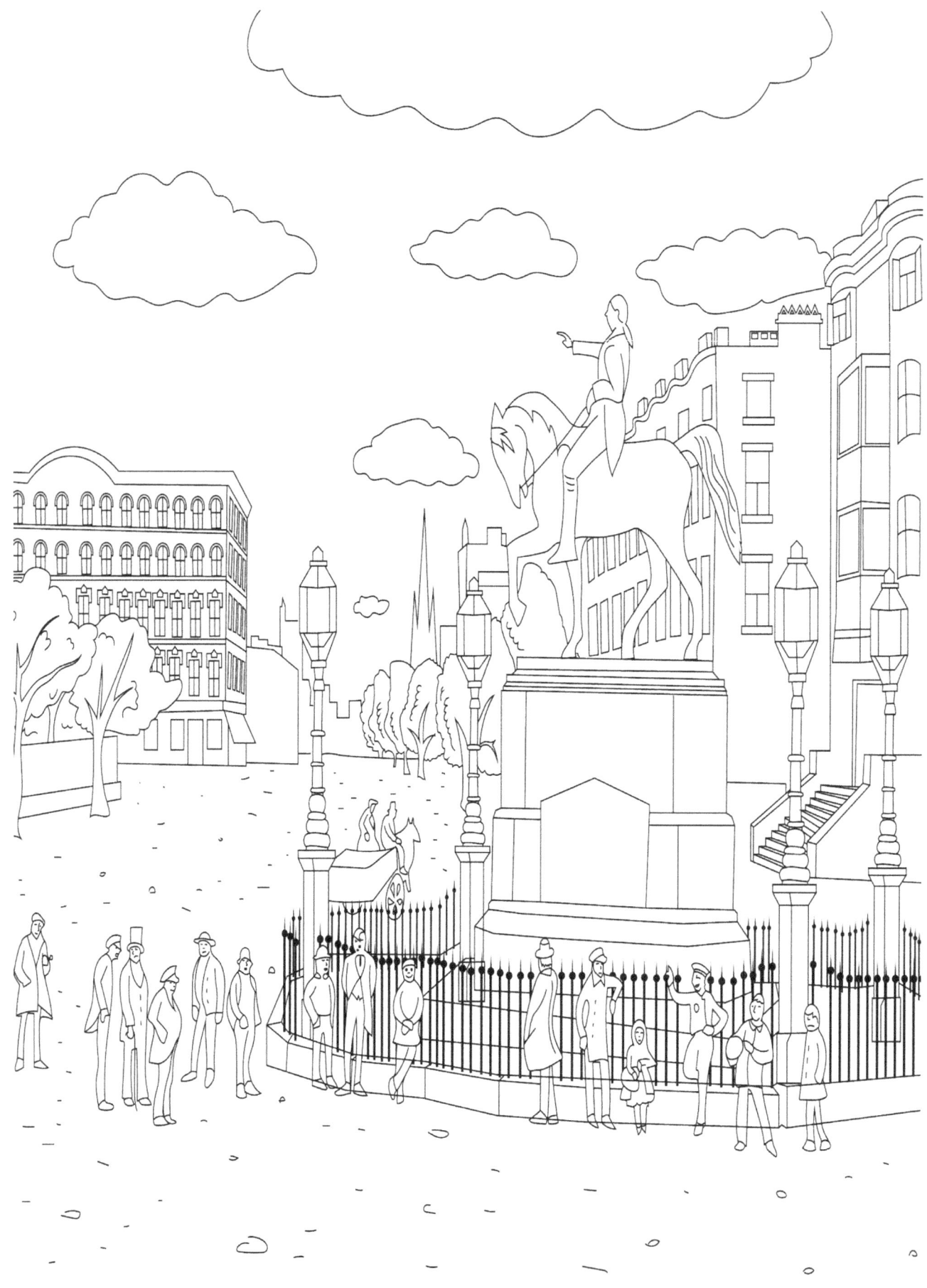

The New York City
Department of Parks and Recreation

This New York government department is maintains the parks system, furnishes recreational opportunities for residents and visitors, and preserves and maintains the ecological diversity of the natural areas, around 30,000 acres.

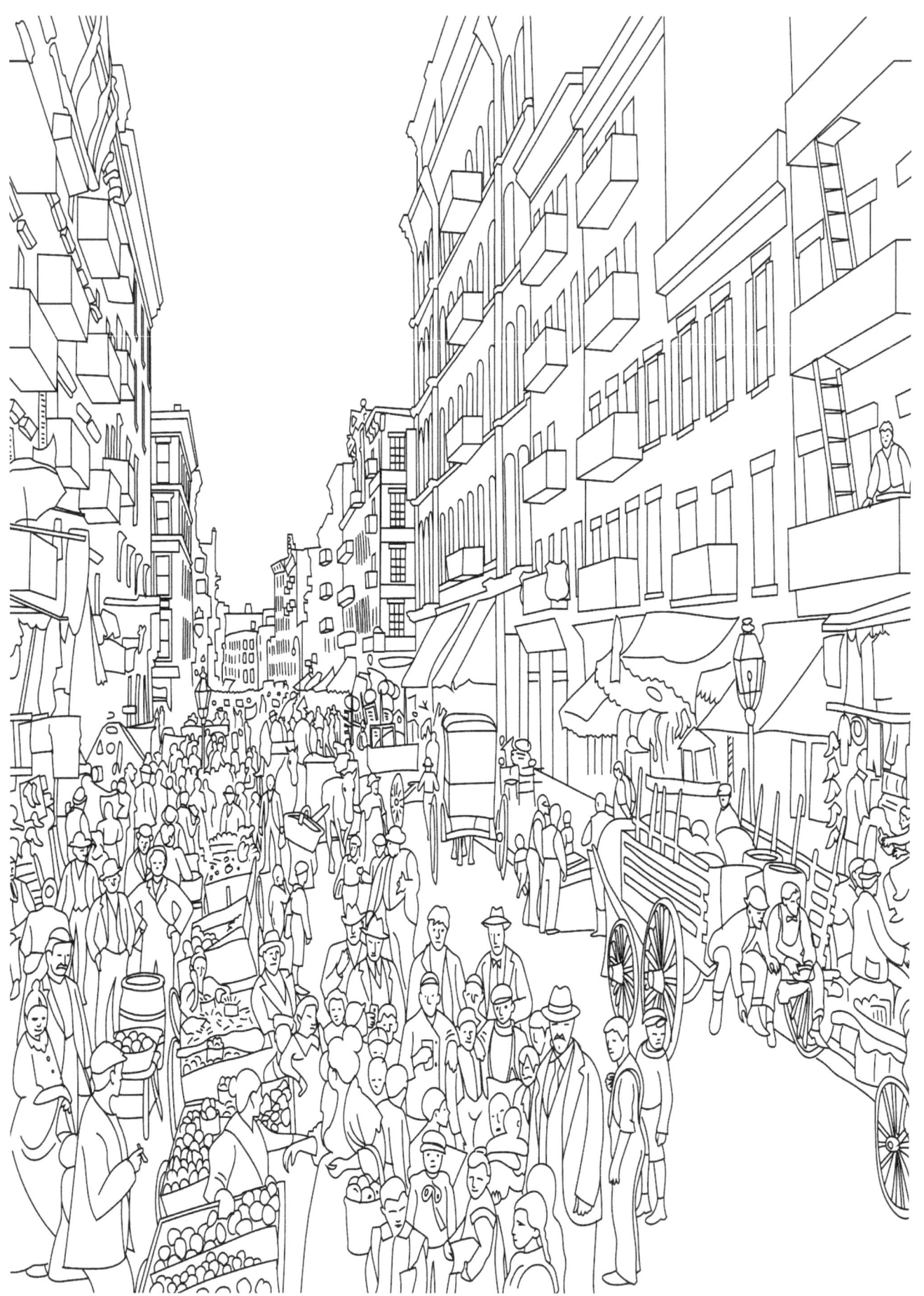

Busy New York

New York dominated the USA with its communications, trade, finance, popular culture and high culture from 1890-1930. It also had more than a fourth of the 300 largest corporations headquartered there.

Around 1898, Brooklyn and Manhattan consolidated to form the modern City of New York, which was made up of the Bronx borough, the Borough of Queens and the Borough of Richmond.

The Bronx saw their population grow from 200,000 in 1900 to 1.3 million in 1930. New York City was ranked as the most populous city in the world in 1925, overtaking even London, and maintained that glory for a century.

Throughout the first half of the 20th century, the city became a world center for industry, commerce, and communication, marking its rising influence with such events as the Hudson-Fulton Celebration of 1909. Interborough Rapid Transit (the first New York City Subway company) began operating in 1904, and the railroads operating out of Grand Central Terminal and Pennsylvania Station thrived.

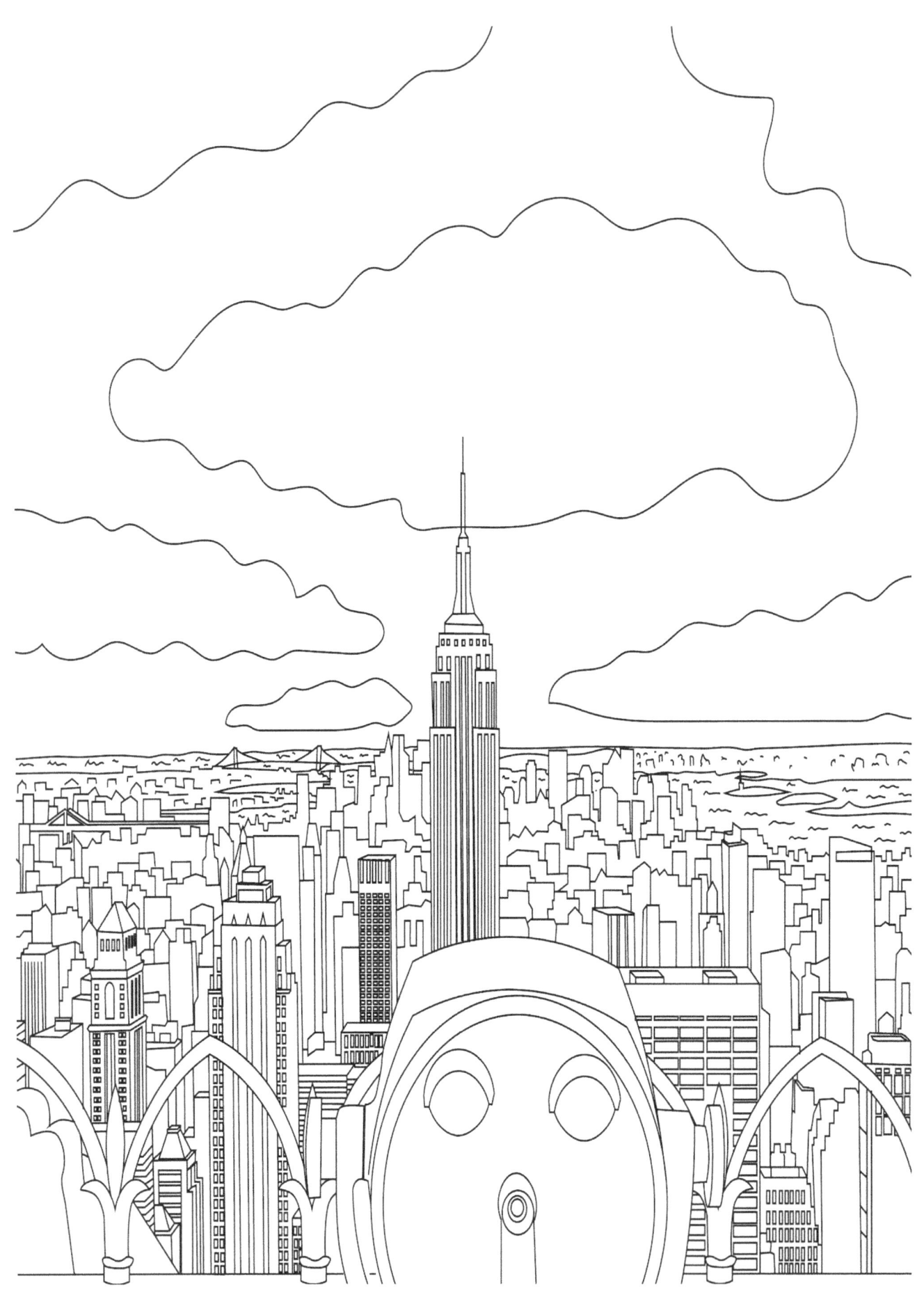

The Empire State Building

This iconic Empire State building was once the world's tallest building from 1931-1970. Standing at 102 stories high, it is located in Manhattan, New York and received its nickname from the Empire State, New York. Currently it is the fifth-tallest skyscraper in the United States and the 35th tallest in the world.

As an American cultural icon, the Empire State building was designed in the Art Deco style and was also named one of the Seven Wonders of the Modern World. The New York City Board of Estimate confirmed the building and its street floor interior as landmarks of the New York City Landmarks Preservation Commission. In 1986, it became a National Historic Landmark and the AIA's List of America's Favorite Architecture ranked it as number one in 2007.

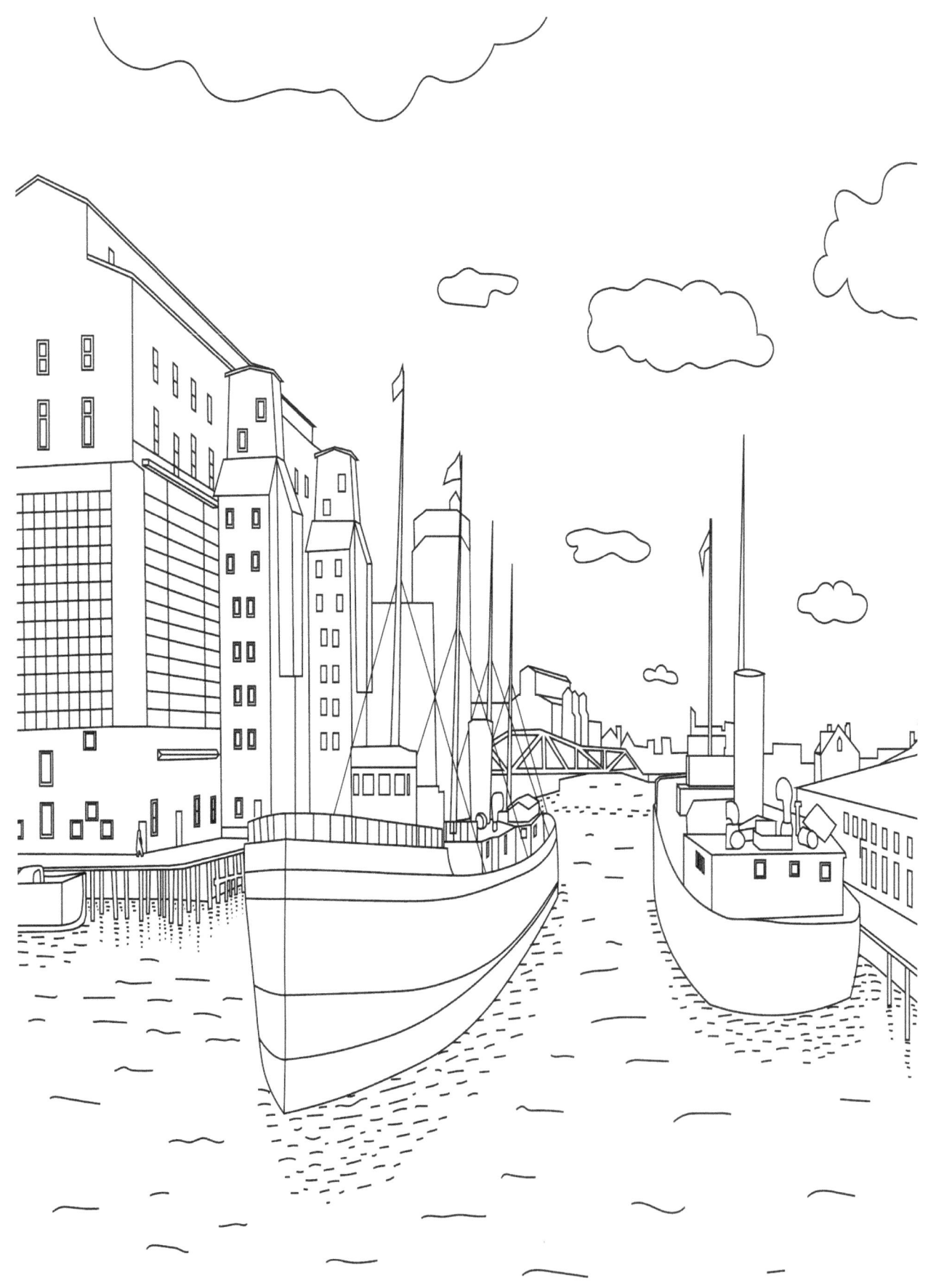

The New York Harbor

Passage to the New York Harbor was shallow and complex, requiring loaded ships to wait outside the harbor until high tide. From the many difficulties and navigation struggles ships had, New York required the ships to be guided by an experienced pilot. Until in 1808, United States Coast Surveyor, Lieutenant Thomas Gedney, discovered a new and deeper channel through Narrows. This new channel was 2 feet deeper, which was enough for fully laden ships to pass into the harbor even during slack tide.

The first American dry-dock was completed in 1824 on the East River and grew rapidly due to the introduction of steamships. Then in 1825, the Erie Canal was built, and became the most important trans-shipping port between America, Europe and other coasts.

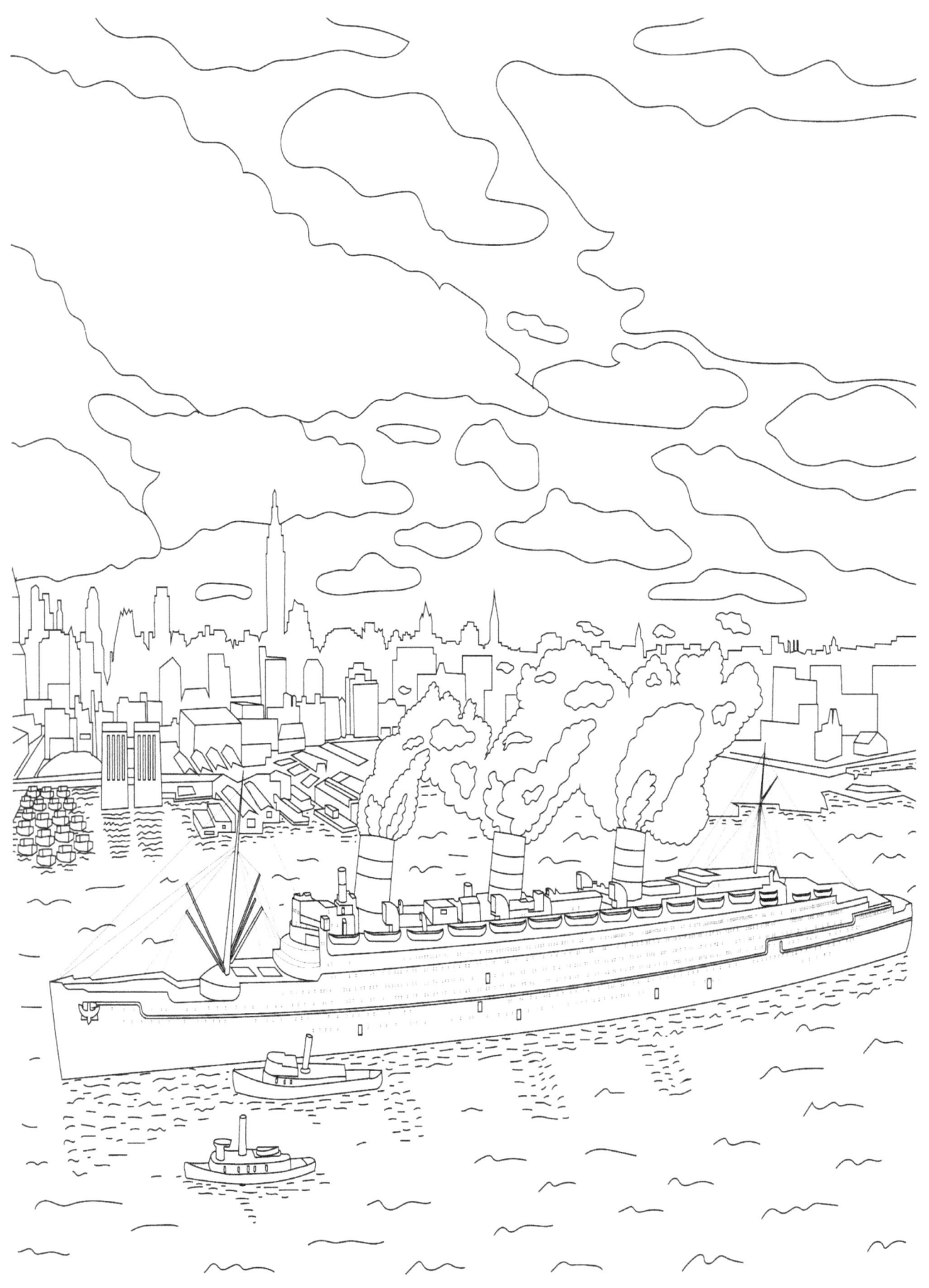

The Queen

Queen Mary was the new liner launched in 1934 by Queen Mary. She had eighteen drag chains to check the progress into the Clyde, a widened portion in the *slipway* to accommodate the launch.

Sir Edgar T. Britten was the master designate for Cunard White Star while the ship was under construction and was also commander on ship during the voyage from Southampton, England in May 27, 1936. She sailed at high speeds during the voyage to New York, until she came upon a heavy fog, requiring her to slow down. Nevertheless, she arrived at the New York Harbor on June 1, 1936.

The Queen Mary was criticized as being too traditional and just an enlarged version of her Cunard predecessors from the pre-World War I era. She had a gross tonnage of 80,774 and proved to be more popular than her larger rival, by carrying more passengers.

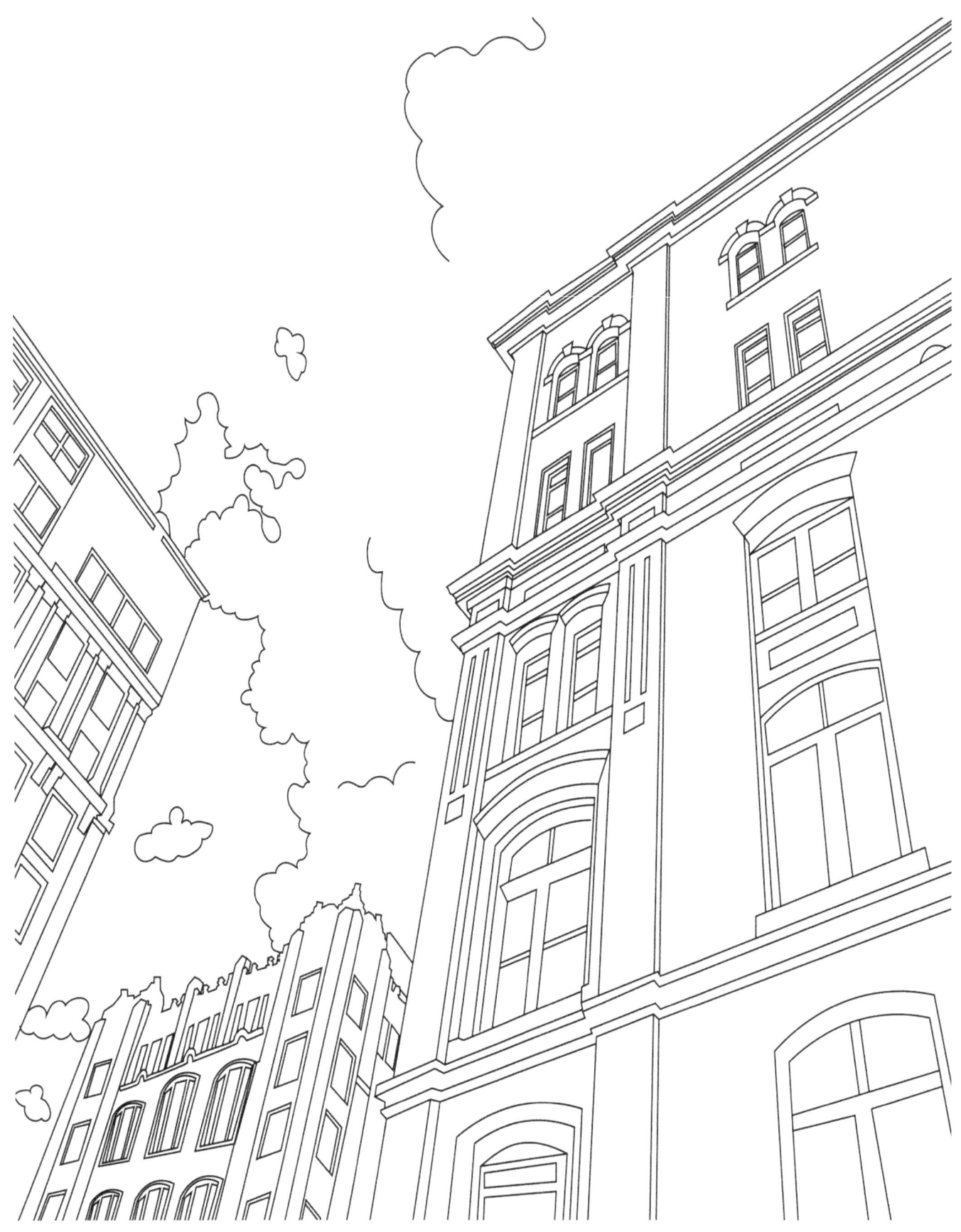

New York Buildings

In the American cities of New York City and Chicago, the early skyscrapers were a range of tall, commercial buildings built between 1884 and 1939.

Traditionally, cities were made up of low-rise buildings, but after the Civil War the United States saw a significant growth and the development of taller buildings began. Improvements in technology included fireproofed, iron-framed structures with deep foundations, and new inventions such as the elevator and electric lighting were introduced to building plans.

New York began to experiment with designs and came up with iconic buildings such as the Flatiron, the Singer Tower (612 feet), the Metropolitan Life Insurance Company Tower (700 feet) and the Woolworth Building (792 feet).

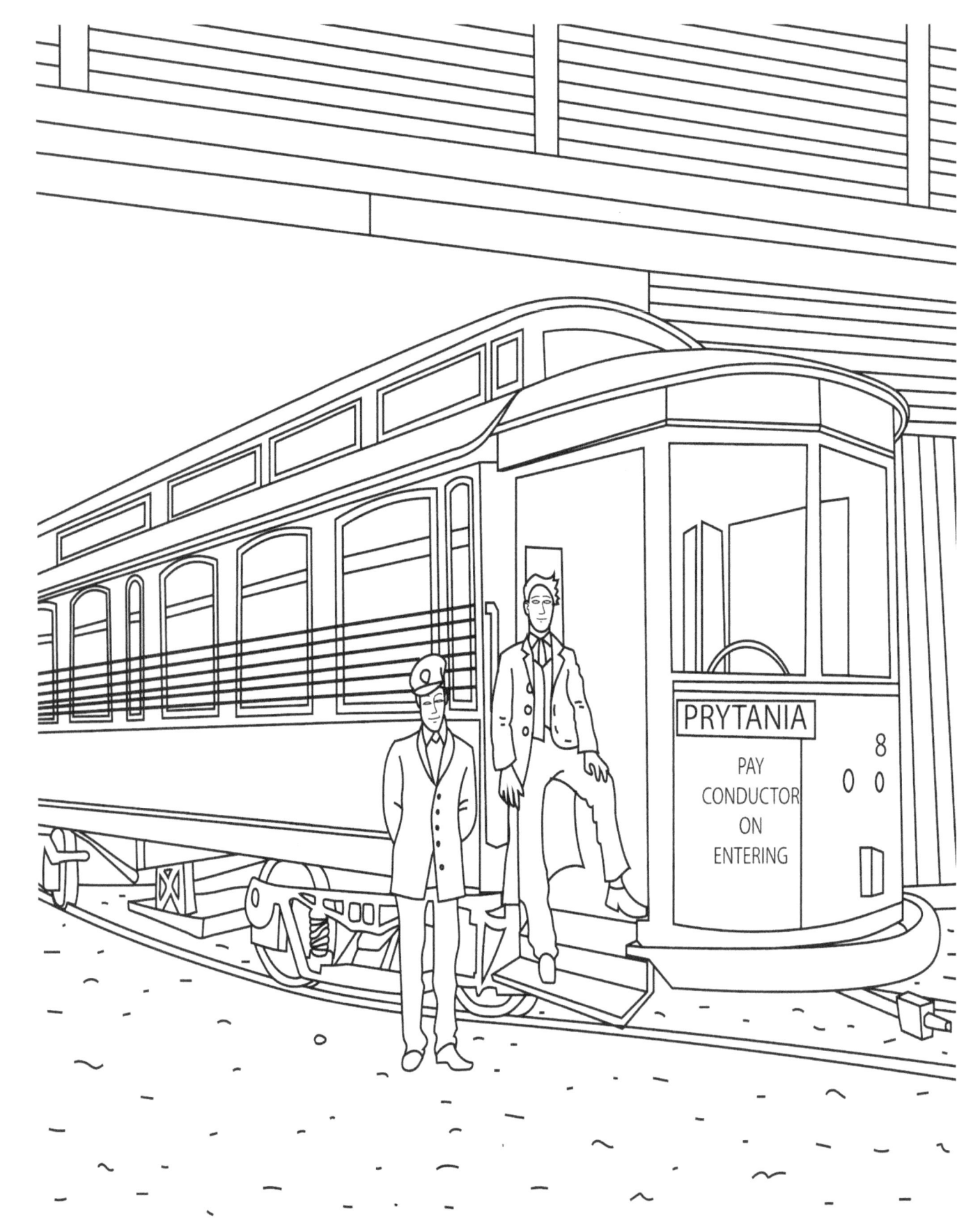

Steam Train

Charles Harvey and his West Side and Yonkers Patent Railway company constructed the first elevated Manhattan (New York County) railroad line from 1867-1870. These steam railroads were popular among the areas with fewer waterways. As populations grew, railroads were elevated or depressed to escape road traffic. The railroads soon became electric due to the complaints of soot and occasional flaming ember showers from overhead steam locomotives.

New York, Kings and Richmond Counties and other cities, towns and villages consolidated to make the City of Greater New York in 1898. During this time the people wanted to have rapid transit from underground subways, but no company was willing to take on the project due to the amount of capital required to build.

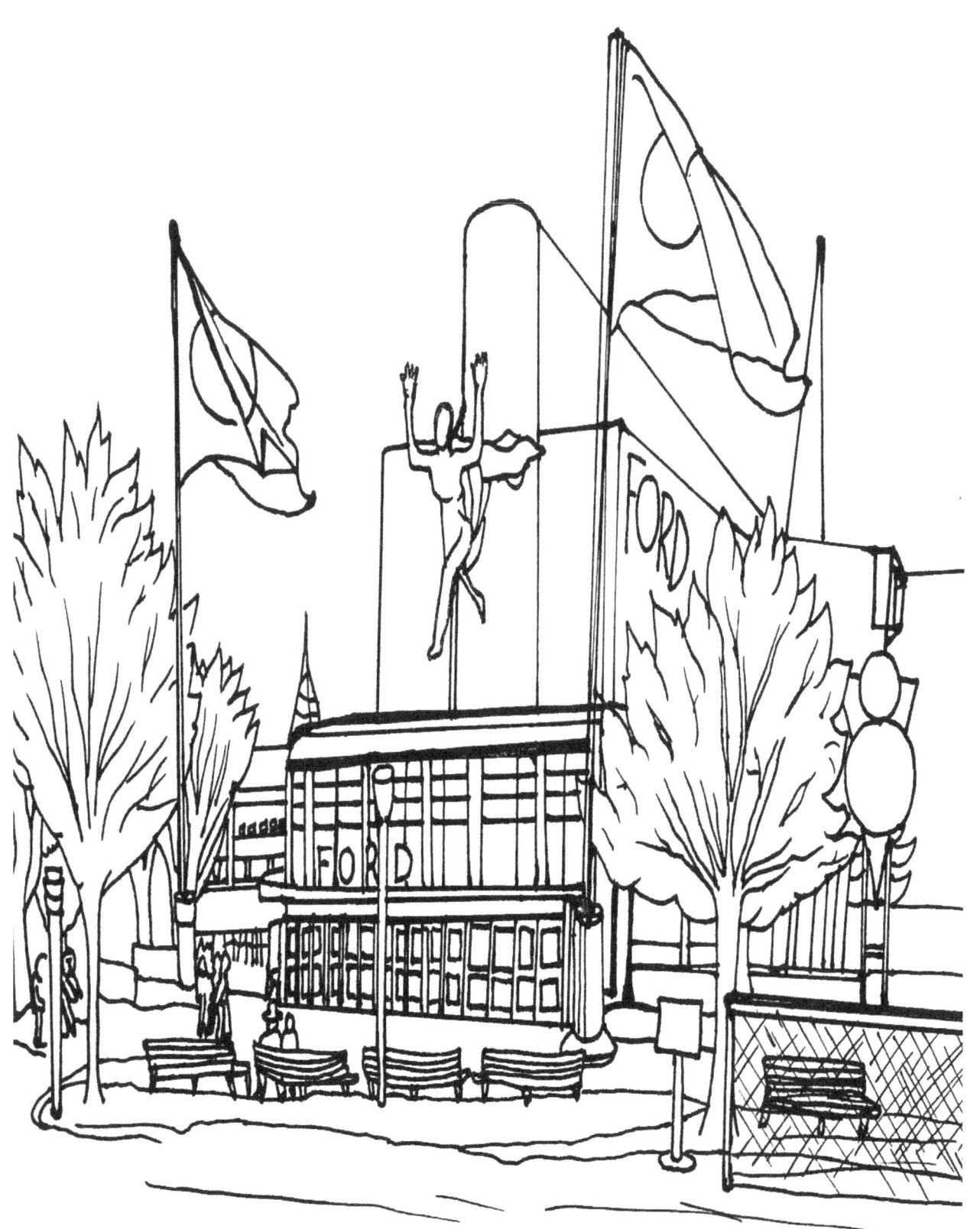

The 1939 New York World's Fair

In 1939, the theme of the World's Fair in New York was "The World of Tomorrow". The planning committee was given permission to develop on the site of a former ash dump on 1,200 acres in Queens. Extraordinary pavilions and exhibitions were built from government agencies, corporations, civic groups and other organizations.

Structures like the iconic Tylon and Perisphere became symbols of the entire fair, housing a diorama called "Democracity," the utopian city of the future.

The entertainments varied from marionette shows and thrill rides to girlie shows and choreographed aquatic extravaganzas and were enjoyed by 44 million people over the course of two seasons.